# Contents

## Check on the chicks!
**Focus on: ch** as in <u>ch</u>ip ......................................... 3

## Shep and me
**Focus on: sh** as in <u>sh</u>op ................................... 8

## What is that thing?
**Focus on: th, wh, ph**
as in <u>th</u>ing, <u>wh</u>en, <u>ph</u>one ............................... 16

**Phonemes:** ch, sh, th, wh, ph
**'Tricky' word:** my

# About this book

These short stories are designed to give children blending and reading practice. They are decodable, which means the words in them only include letter shapes and sounds that the children have learned. The stories gradually introduce 'tricky' words, building on the learning in the Red Series.

The progression links directly to the teaching order in the Letterland teaching range. Each story begins with a title page that provides important information for children and teachers.

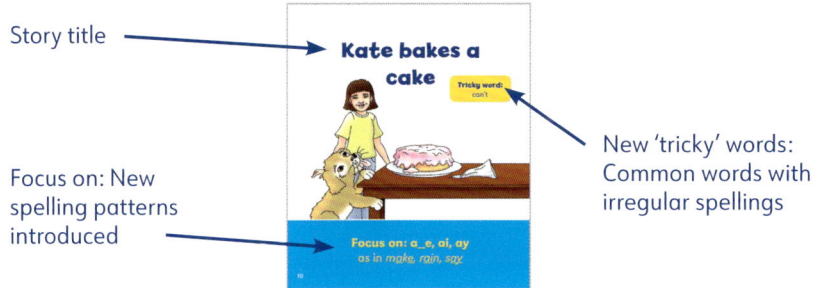

Story title

Focus on: New spelling patterns introduced

New 'tricky' words: Common words with irregular spellings

**Basic teaching tips:**

- Encourage the sounding out of decodable words (and any decodable parts of 'tricky' words).
- Discuss the stories with the children to ensure comprehension and engagement.
- Encourage re-reading in pairs or individually to develop fluency and reading for meaning.

**Red Series** introduces the a-z letters and sounds and some 'tricky words'. On completion of this series, the following words remain tricky in part: **a, the, she, oh, for, that, ok, they, says, her, this, to, said, of, what, you, was, want, come, sees, asks, do.** These words are included in **Blue Series**.

# Check on the chicks!

**Focus on: ch** as in *chip*

He checks on the pen.
He sees the chicks on the run.

He picks up the chicks and puts them back in the pen.

Then he chops the logs.

He had such a lot to chop.
He rests on the logs.

# Shep and me

**Tricky word:** my

**Focus on: sh** as in *shop*

I got Shep at the pet shop.
Shep licks me!

He naps in that shed.
Hush!

Then he gets up.
Sit up, Shep. That's it!

Shep has a big dish.
Shep wants to see lots.

He wants to see the ships, the shells, and the fish in the shops.

I hug Shep.
He licks my chin!

This is my dog Shep.
He is lots of fun.

# What is that thing?

**Focus on: th, wh , ph**
as in _<u>th</u>ing, <u>wh</u>en, <u>ph</u>one_

What is that thing?
I think that is a fin.

It's a dolphin!
What is that thing next to the dolphin?
It has thick legs.

It's just Ed splashing!
What is that thing next to Ed?

It's just the duck!
"Thanks!" said the duck
when she got wet.

What is that odd thing on the sand?
It has thin legs and lots of them.

What *is* this odd thing?
Can you help?

# About this series

This series of 10 books accompanies the Letterland teaching range. Each book contains a selection of short stories. In total there are 32 engaging stories featuring the phonic elements listed below as well as some 'tricky' high-frequency words.

| Book | Focus elements | As in the word... | Story titles |
|---|---|---|---|
| 1 | sh, ch, th, th, wh, ph | chip, shop, that, thing | Check on the chicks / Shep and me / What is that thing? |
| 2 | a_e, ai, ay | make, rain, say, | A safe place / Kate bakes a cake / Kane's tail! |
| 3 | e_e, ea, ee, y | these, sea, bee, baby | A trip to the sea / Mr E's trees / Happy! |
| 4 | i_e, ie, igh, y | like, tie, night, my | Ben rides his bike / Cats at night / What a mess! |
| 5 | o_e, oa, ow | home, boat, show | The bad goat / When the cold wind blows / Lost in the Queen's maze |
| 6 | u_e, ue, oo, ew | cube, blue, moon, few, grew | Stuck on a dune / A day at the zoo / The Hat Man's new roof |
| 7 | ar, or, er, ir, ur, wr | farm, for, her, girl, fur, write | The big match / Snapshots / The bird girls / My very bad morning |
| 8 | o, oo, u, oy, oi | son, book, put, boy, coin | Oscar's brother / The big pull / Nick's noisy new toy |
| 9 | aw, au, ow, ou | saw, cause, how, out, | Draw it! / The house mouse / Look now! |
| 10 | Review ear, air | pear, year, fair | My shark dream / A fresh feast / Bears at the fair / A fairy story |

# Collect the sets

## Phonics Readers - Red Series

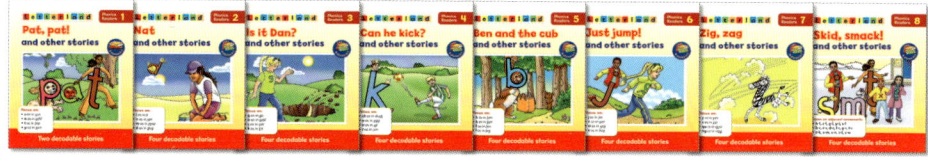

## Phonics Readers - Blue Series

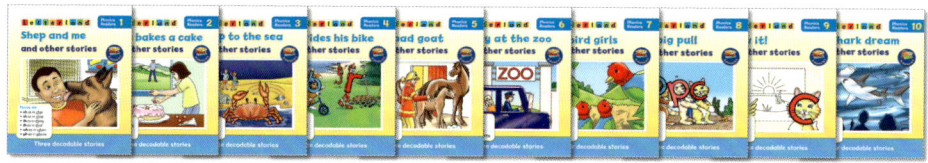

Published by Letterland International Ltd. 8/10 South Street, Epsom, Surrey, KT18 7PF, UK.
www.letterland.com
ISBN: 978-1-78248-180-5
Product Code: TJ02

© Letterland International 2016
LETTERLAND™ is a trademark of Letterland International Ltd.

First published 2013. This new edition published 2016.
Reprinted 2023.
10 9 8 7 6 5 4 3 2

Authors: Stamey Carter and Lisa Holt
Originator of Letterland: Lyn Wendon
Artwork: Baz Rowell
Design: Lisa Holt

The author asserts the moral right to be identified as the author of this work. All rights reserved. No part of this publication may be reproduced, stored in a retrieval system, or transmitted in any form or by any means, electronic, mechanical, photocopying, recording or otherwise, without either the prior permission of the Publisher or a licence permitting restricted copying in the United Kingdom issued by the Copyright Licensing Agency Ltd, 90 Tottenham Court Road, London W1T 4LP. This book is sold subject to the condition that it shall not be way of trade or otherwise be lent, hired out or otherwise circulated without the Publisher's prior consent.

Printed in Beirut, Lebanon.